A PRISONER'S CHRISTIANITY

ANDREW WOODROW

A PRISONER'S CHRISTIANITY

ANDREW WOODROW

5317 Wye Creek Dr, Frederick, MD 21703-6938
Website: newcovenantmedia.com
Email: info@newcovenantmedia.com
Phone: 301-473-8781 or 800-376-4146
Fax: 240-206-0373

A PRISONER'S CHRISTIANITY

Copyright 2008 © by Andrew Woodrow

Published by: New Covenant Media
                  5317 Wye Creek Drive
                  Frederick, Maryland 21703-6938

Orders: www.newcovenantmedia.com

All rights reserved. No part of this publication may be reproduced, stored in a retrieval system, or transmitted in any form by any means, electronic, mechanical, photocopy, recording, or otherwise without the prior permission of the publisher, except as provided by USA copyright law.

Printed in the United States of America

ISBN 13: 978-1-928965-29-9

Scripture quotations are taken from the HOLY BIBLE, NEW INTERNATIONAL VERSION®. Copyright © 1973, 1978, 1984 International Bible Society. Used by permission of Zondervan. All rights reserved.

DEDICATION

To my friends
Frank Robertson and Rowland Hill;
with thanks for their help
and encouragement.

TABLE OF CONTENTS

TABLE OF CONTENTS	I
INTRODUCTION	III
SIN	1
JESUS CHRIST	9
SAVING FAITH	15
CONVERSION	21
REPENTANCE	27
THE FIGHT OF FAITH	33
LIVING AS DISCIPLES	39
THE HOLY SPIRIT	45
THE KINGDOM OF GOD	51
THE WORD OF GOD	55
GOD	63
NOTHING IS HIDDEN: A CONFESSION	71

INTRODUCTION

A Prisoner's Christianity is written for prisoners, by a prisoner. I have spent the last eighteen years in New Jersey prisons, serving a thirty-year sentence for murder. By God's mercy I have been a Christian for most of that time, and in one sense this book is my story. When writing about "Sin", "Repentance", "The Fight of Faith", etc., I am writing from experience. And because I have experienced these things in prison I hope I can share something with others in prison.

Let me confess that I am guilty of my crimes. I am guilty and I deserve my sentence, and worse. This book is written for people who deserve to be in prison. This is not a book about getting out of jail by faith. It is a book about knowing God's salvation, and living by faith even while behind prison bars.

Although this is written from experience, it is not a "story." It is a book of doctrine. I know this may turn some people off. We often hear that we need "Christ, not doctrine; salvation, not religion." I understand that. But what we believe about Christ and salvation is still very important. We believe in the Christ and the salvation taught in the Bible—and the Bible teaches doctrine. The Bible tells us to guard doctrine carefully: "…encourage others by sound doctrine and refute those who oppose it" (Tit. 1:9b).

That is why I have written this book. I am afraid that prisoners are taught little sound doctrine. Prison ministries stick to the basics, for good reason. But the result is that prison churches and Christians are often shallow. We are not firmly rooted, as we need to be. To become firmly rooted we must understand our faith. We need doctrine. So I have tried to share this simply and briefly, with some comments especially for prisoners.

Finally, let me say that Jesus viewed prisoners as special objects of his love and concern. Talking about the Day of Judgment, he said, "'Then the King will say to those on his right, "Come, you who are blessed by my Father; take your inheritance, the kingdom prepared for you since the creation of the world. For I was hungry and you gave me something to eat, I was thirsty and you gave me something to drink, I was a stranger and you invited me in, I needed clothes and you clothed me, I was sick and you looked after me, *I was in prison and you came to visit me.*"… I tell you the truth, whatever you did for one of the least of these brothers of mine, you did for me'" (Mt. 25:34-36, 40 emphasis added).

I think that Jesus showed a special love for prisoners because prison pictures the condition of all people before God. Right now this world is a prison where sinners are kept from the freedom and blessedness of the kingdom of God. The only hope for any "prisoner" is the gospel of Jesus Christ. So, while this book is meant for those in prisons, I believe it has an application for all men. The things demanded of prisoners are the same things demanded of all people. Prisoners are not as different from others as many seem to think.

May God bless this book and its readers, to his glory.

> "EVERYONE WHO SINS BREAKS THE LAW;
> IN FACT, SIN IS LAWLESSNESS."
> (1 JOHN 3:4)

SIN

Beginning with Sin

The Bible gives this definition of sin: "Everyone who sins breaks the law; in fact, sin is lawlessness" (1 Jn. 3:4). Sin is breaking God's law. When we do what God tells us not to do, or when we do not do what he tells us to do, we sin.

SIN belongs in capital letters; it is not just a minor "technicality." It should be known as it really is. It ruins life. That is why the first thing to look at in this study is sin. This is where people begin their walk with Jesus. Until we know the truth of sin, any religion, or no religion, will do. But when we see sin for what it is a new concern will arise in the soul. That concern will only be quieted when the soul rests through faith in the work of Jesus Christ.

Origin of Sin

The first three chapters of the Bible tell us about the origin of sin. Genesis, chapter one, looks at the creation of all things by God: "God saw all that he had made, and it was very good…" In chapter two, we see the creation of the first people, Adam and Eve, and the Garden of Eden where they lived. It was a beautiful life in every way, where they were in perfect harmony with God. God gave them only one law: he said, "… 'You are free to eat from any tree in the garden;

but you must not eat from the tree of the knowledge of good and evil, for when you eat of it you will surely die'" (Gen 2:16-17). Chapter three recounts to us the first sin and its results. Adam and Eve broke the law and ate of the forbidden tree. For this God made them subject to death as he had warned, and banished them from the garden.

We have all heard this story and for that reason we might overlook the lesson about sin. Sin separated Adam and Eve from God. Instead of loving God perfectly, they chose to rebel against him, and they lost the beauty and blessing of Paradise. Sin is offensive to God and he will not let it exist in his presence. God is holy and anything that is marked by sin must be separated from him: "...God is light; in him there is no darkness at all," and he is "too pure to look on evil..." (1 Jn. 1:5; Hab. 1:13). Even Adam and Eve, who were made in his image to rule over his creation, had to be put out of his presence, because of SIN.

More than this, through Adam sin entered into the whole human race. God put Adam and Eve out of his presence, marked by sin and subject to death. In that condition they became the first parents of mankind. "...sin entered the world through one man, and death through sin, and in this way death came to all men, because all sinned" and, "...all have sinned and fall short of the glory of God" (Rom. 5:12; 3:23).

What this means is that our lives are wrong from birth. We are the children of fallen sinners. By nature we break God's laws, and experience guilt for sin. We rebel against God and we experience suffering and death. We do not now live in the 'kingdom of God', but are separated from his presence. We are *sinners*.

God's Anger with Sin

In Genesis, chapters 6 and 7 we learn about the flood of Noah. At that point eight or nine generations had lived outside of God's presence after Adam and Eve's fall. In that short time mankind had grown worse and worse. It is written, "The LORD saw how great man's wickedness on the earth had become, and that every inclination of the thoughts of his heart was only evil all the time" (Gen. 6:5). *Every* inclination was *only* evil, *all* the time.

The result of this was that "the LORD was grieved that he had made man on the earth, and his heart was filled with pain" (Gen. 6:6). God sent a flood, and "every living thing that moved on the earth perished..." (Gen. 7:21). Only Noah was shown mercy by God; he and his family were spared.

Once again, we know this story, and we are likely to pass it over without really thinking about its lesson on sin. If we do stop and think, we see a terrifying message. First we see how quickly the disease of sin spread. Then we see how God hated it. His response was to punish it, and the punishment that he brought was death. It may be hard to imagine God showing such anger and killing all the people except Noah and his family. But that is what we see. The flood teaches us the painful lesson that because of SIN, God is angry with men, and he will punish them for their sin.

Israel's Example

After the flood, God filled the earth with people again through Noah's family. He then began to give his law to men in greater detail. Much of the Old Testament is a record of God's law given to the nation of Israel, and of Israel's response to it. Through Israel's example, the Bible continues to tell the story of man's sin and God's anger toward sin.

The clearest record of this law was the Ten Commandments. God said:

> 'I am the LORD your God, who brought you out of Egypt, out of the land of slavery.
>
> 'You shall have no other gods before me.
>
> 'You shall not make for yourself an idol in the form of anything in heaven above or on the earth beneath or in the Waters below. You shall not bow down to them or worship them...
>
> 'You shall not misuse the name of the Lord your God...
>
> 'Remember the Sabbath day by keeping it holy...
>
> 'Honor your father and your mother...
>
> 'You shall not murder.
>
> 'You shall not commit adultery.
>
> 'You shall not steal.
>
> 'You shall not give false testimony against your neighbor.
>
> 'You shall not covet...' (Ex. 20:2-17)

"Sin is lawlessness." God presented man with law, and the record shows that the law proved man's sin. Man could not keep the law. Man is fallen in sin and breaks God's laws and arouses his anger. God finally sent Israel into captivity in Babylon, with this explanation: "... 'Great is the LORD'S anger that burns against us because our fathers have not obeyed the words of this book...'" (2 Kg. 22:13).

Sin

Jesus' Teachings

When Jesus came he taught that God's law is higher even than the Old Testament law had revealed. For instance, he said, "'you have heard that it was said, "Do not commit adultery." But I tell you that anyone who looks at a woman lustfully has already committed adultery with her in his heart'" (Mt. 5:27-28). Throughout his "Sermon on the Mount" (Mt. 5-7), Jesus showed us that God's law judges the heart. He taught that thoughts and feelings are as important as actions, and that God's law covers what happens inside of us as well as what happens on the outside.

Jesus also commanded that we "'be perfect, therefore, as your heavenly Father is perfect'" (Mt. 5:48). According to Jesus, God's law demands that we be perfect in thought, word, and deed.

Despite this high view of the law, Jesus knew that "…sin is lawlessness" (1 Jn 3:4), and that God would punish sin. He warned that "'…the fire of hell'" (Mt. 18:9) awaited sinners. He spoke of his final judgment of sinners. He said: "'The Son of Man will send out his angels, and they will weed out of his kingdom everything that causes sin and all who do evil. They will throw them into the fiery furnace, where there will be weeping and gnashing of teeth'" (Mt. 13:41, 42).

The Bible's message has not changed. Mankind is fallen in sin. We are not perfect as we should be; we break God's law. There will be a day of final judgment when sin will be punished. The conclusion is that SIN costs mankind Paradise with God, and it gives us Hell instead.

Honesty about Sin

Fellow prisoners, you surely think about your sin. You think about how you came to be where you are. You think about your rebellion against your family, your community, and against God himself. You think about your crimes and about your bad decisions and wasted chances in life. We all do.

We need to think about what this really means. We must know that sin is the worst thing in the world. Our greatest need is not to be free from prison or from our present trials. Our greatest need is to be free from sin. We need to be forgiven by God. We need to be accepted by him instead of condemned by his law. We need to be moved out from under God's anger and back into the good and innocent standing of Adam and Eve before the fall. Every other desire of our life is nothing compared to this great need.

If we see this to be our great need, we will confess before God that we are fallen sinners, who deserve his wrath; his law is good, but we have broken it; we have been rebels against him. We have followed Adam and Eve in sin and we have ruined ourselves. Even more than a prison sentence, we deserve Hell for our sins. This may be painful, and humbling, and even frightening to experience, but it will be seeing SIN as God sees it. It will be *honest*. And if we will deal with sin in honesty, it will be the starting point for a new life. It will be the beginning of a blessed change and true Christianity.

> "...WHEN THE TIME HAD FULLY COME, GOD SENT HIS SON,
> BORN OF A WOMAN,
> BORN UNDER THE LAW,
> TO REDEEM THOSE UNDER THE LAW,
> THAT WE MIGHT RECEIVE THE FULL RIGHTS OF SONS."
> (GALATIANS 4:4, 5)

JESUS CHRIST

The Way of Salvation

In the first chapter we looked at sin. Sin is the ruin of man. Mankind is fallen in sin and God's anger is upon him. The situation seems hopeless.

Despite the ruin of sin, the Bible is full of the message of God's love for man—for sinners. Wherever we look in the Bible we see that there are those with whom God deals as his children and his people. We may say that one of the reasons God gave us the Bible is to tell us how to be changed from being his enemies in sin to become his children. This is the gospel; the good news for sinners that God has made a way of salvation from sin.

This way of salvation is in Jesus Christ, the son of God: "...when the time had fully come, God sent his Son, born of a woman, born under the law, to redeem those under the law, that we might receive the full rights of sons" (Gal. 4:4, 5).

We will now look at Jesus Christ in three ways. First, as he was "born of a woman", we will see a unique man who was not fallen by nature, but who was always holy. Second, as he was "born under the law", we will see a man who never sinned and broke the law, but who always did God's will. And third, as he came "to redeem those under the law", we will see a man who suffered God's punishment, even though he never sinned. He suffered this on the behalf of others who had broken the law, in order to redeem them, or to pay for their sins.

The Son

Jesus Christ was "born of a woman" just like us, but he was also very different from us. The angel Gabriel was sent to a virgin named Mary and said: "'…Mary, you have found favor with God. You will be with child and give birth to a son, and you are to give him the name Jesus. He will be great and will be called the Son of the Most High… The Holy Spirit will come upon you, and the power of the Most High will overshadow you. So the Holy one to be born will be called the Son of God'" (Lk. 1:30-32, 35).

Later an angel also appeared to Mary's betrothed husband Joseph. "All this took place to fulfill what the Lord has said through the prophet: 'The virgin will be with child and will give birth to a son, and they will call him Immanuel'—which means, 'God with us'" (Mt. 1:22, 23).

Jesus was not another fallen man. The Holy Spirit put Jesus within the virgin. He was not born with a sinful nature, as are other men. Instead, he had God's own holy nature; God himself was with us in the Son.

The Servant

Jesus was "born under the law" like us. But he was different from us because he lived without sin, and did the will of God always and perfectly.

When he was an adult he was baptized. "As Jesus was coming up out of the water, he saw heaven being torn open and the Spirit descending on him like a dove. And a voice came from heaven: 'You are my Son, whom I love; with you I am well pleased'" (Mk. 1:10, 11).

Jesus' public work then began. He called disciples to follow him. He drove out evil spirits, and healed many diseased folks. He ruled over the powers of nature and creation. He taught new laws with authority. He forgave sins and did great works within souls. He acted with an amazing grace and power. With a word or a touch, he did whatever he wanted. Even his closest disciples had to say, "… 'What kind of man is this?…'" (Mt. 8:27).

After doing this work for about three years, Jesus asked his disciples who they thought he was: "Simon Peter answered, 'You are the Christ, the Son of the living God.' Jesus replied, 'Blessed are you, Simon son of Jonah, for this was not revealed to you by man, but by my Father in heaven'" (Mt. 16:16).

It was clear to his followers; Jesus' work made sense because he was not just a man. He was the Christ; the long awaited Servant of God. In conclusion to this, Jesus revealed his glory to three disciples: "There he was transfigured before them. His face shone like the sun, and his clothes became as white as the light…a bright cloud enveloped them, and a voice from the cloud said, 'This is my Son, whom I love; with him I am well pleased. Listen to him!'" (Mt. 17:2, 5).

God marked both the beginning and the end of Jesus Christ's work with the message that he loved the Son and was pleased with him. Jesus the Servant never broke the law of God, so he was not under God's anger for sin. He lived in perfect fellowship with God and always did his will.

The Savior

Jesus Christ came "to redeem those that are born under law…" (Gal. 4:5). As his life came to an end, he especially fulfilled this duty as Savior.

The Bible records the events of Jesus' death in detail. He knew what was coming. He struggled with God in prayer; but in love for the Father and for his disciples, he faced the suffering set before him. He was betrayed and arrested. He was mocked, beaten, spit upon, whipped, and condemned. He was nailed to a cross in pain and shame. But he forgave his murderers. He promised a dying sinner paradise with him. He committed his spirit to the Father and died.

Before he suffered these things, Jesus explained his role as Savior to the disciples at the last supper: "…Jesus took bread, gave thanks and broke it, and gave it to his disciples, saying, 'Take and eat; this is my body.' Then he took the cup, gave thanks and offered it to them, saying, 'Drink from it, all of you. This is my blood of the covenant, which is poured out for many for the forgiveness of sins'" (Mt. 26:26-28).

He showed them that he came to die for sinners as a sacrifice in their stead. Those who trusted in him would be forgiven of their sins and no longer condemned. These would have a new covenant with God, a new standing with God, joined to his perfect Son and Servant. They would be redeemed by the Savior's holy blood.

As a final proof of Jesus' work as Savior, three days after his death, he rose from the grave. Women went to the tomb where Jesus' body was buried. They found the tomb empty, and angels gave them this message: "… 'Why do you look for the living among the dead? He is not here; he is risen!…'" (Lk. 24:5, 6). Jesus then showed himself alive to many of his disciples. He taught them that his life and death and resurrection fulfilled all things. He said the message of the whole Bible was that "… 'The Christ will suffer and rise from the dead on the third day, and repentance and forgiveness of sins will be preached in his name to all nations, beginning at Jerusalem'" (Lk. 24:46, 47).

The Love of God

Once again, prisoners, despite the ruin of sin, the message of God's love for sinners fills the Bible. The gospel is the good news that God has made a way of salvation from sin. This way of salvation is in Jesus Christ, the Son of God. He was a perfect man, without sin, who died on the cross as a sacrifice for sinners. He suffered what sinners deserved. He died for sinners such as us.

We offend God by our sin, but still he loves men. It is amazing, but that is why Jesus came into the world. The Bible says it again and again to be sure it is clear: "But God demonstrates his own love for us in this: While we were still sinners, Christ died for us" (Rom. 5:8). "This is how God showed his love among us: He sent his one and only Son into the world that we might live through him. This is love:

not that we loved God, but that he loved us and sent His Son as an atoning sacrifice for our sins" (1 Jn. 4:9-10).

> **"FOR GOD SO LOVED THE WORLD THAT HE GAVE HIS ONE AND ONLY SON, THAT WHOEVER BELIEVES IN HIM SHALL NOT PERISH BUT HAVE ETERNAL LIFE.'"**
> **(JOHN 3:16)**

SAVING FAITH

Salvation by Faith

In the first two chapters of this book we looked at the ruin of mankind in sin, and at God's way of salvation in Jesus Christ. These are two important truths: We are sinners before God because we break his law. God loves sinners and sent his Son to save them by dying for their sins.

There is a step that we have not discussed. Sinners must enter into God's salvation by *believing* in Jesus Christ. "'For God so loved the world that he gave his one and only Son, that whoever believes in him shall not perish but have eternal life. Whoever believes in him is not condemned, but whoever does not believe stands condemned already because he has not believed in the name of God's one and only Son'" (Jn. 3:16, 18). Faith makes all the difference. Some people believe in the Son of God and are saved, and have eternal life. Some people do not believe in him and are condemned, and perish.

Examples of Faith

The Gospels and the Book of Acts often picture saving faith in Jesus. Men and women are helpless and hopeless until they see Jesus. Then they come to him, put their faith in him, and he saves them.

One example of this is in Mark 5:25-29: "And a woman was there who had been subject to bleeding for twelve years. She had suffered a great deal under the care of many doctors and had spent all she had, yet instead of getting better she grew worse. When she heard about Jesus, she came up behind him in the crowd and touched his cloak, because she thought, 'If I just touch his clothes, I will be healed.' Immediately her bleeding stopped and she felt in her body that she was freed from her suffering." Then, in verse 34, "He said to her, 'Daughter, your faith has healed you. Go in peace and be freed from your suffering'."

Another example is a jailer had hurt some of Jesus' disciples. When he realized his sin, he said to Paul, "'...what must I do to be saved?' [Paul] replied, 'Believe in the Lord Jesus, and you will be saved—you and your household.'...then immediately he and all his family were baptized" (Acts 16:30, 31, 33).

A Personal Relationship with Jesus Christ

To better understand this saving faith, it may help to look again at the Last Supper. As we have seen, "...Jesus took bread, gave thanks and broke it, and gave it to his disciples, saying, 'Take and eat; this is my body.' Then he took the cup, gave thanks and offered it to them, saying, 'Drink from it, all of you. This is my blood of the covenant, which is poured out for many for the forgiveness of sins'" (Mt. 26:26-28).

This points to a spiritual and personal union with Jesus. He enters our life and we begin a 'personal relationship' with him. This is much like a marriage. His blood is his vow of love for us; drinking his blood is our vow of love for him, and, like a marriage, two "become one flesh." We become one with Jesus.

When we enter into this personal relationship with Jesus we enter into 'the new covenant' of God. The important thing about this new covenant is that in it we have "forgiveness of sins." We used to be under the just condemnation of God. This meant that we were condemned as sinners for falling short of God's standards. We stood separated from God because of sin. But now, God has made a new covenant in Jesus' blood. This means that God's righteous standard has been satisfied by Jesus' sacrifice for our sins and we are no longer condemned. We stand forgiven and accepted by God as one with Jesus because of our union with him.

A Warning against Errors

This personal relationship with Jesus is vital; it means life. "Jesus said to them, 'I tell you the truth, unless you eat the flesh of the Son of Man and drink his blood, you have no life in you'" (Jn. 6:53). This is so important that we must beware of errors that keep some people from joining with him in faith.

Jesus often invited people to join with him. He said, "… 'If anyone is thirsty, let him come to me and drink'" and "'Come to me, all you who are weary and burdened, and I will give you rest'" (Jn. 7:37; Mt. 11:28). His invitation was always made freely, to the needy. But many people, even 'Christian' people, do not join with Jesus in saving faith because they do not understand their own *need*, or because they do not understand that salvation is *free*.

First, some never realize they are needy. Their family may be Christian. They may attend a church and be baptized. They may even understand that all people sin and that Jesus is the Savior. But if they do not realize their own sin and their own need they will not join with Jesus. Only the 'thirsty' care to drink—only the 'burdened' care to rest. Only the needy will join with Jesus in a spiritual and personal way.

Second, some do not realize that Jesus' invitation is free. They try to earn their salvation instead of simply receiving it from Christ. They want God to accept them for their works. This takes many forms. Some do penance and become very religious. Some give money or do charity work. But Jesus did not tell us to bring a 'payment' to him. He told us to come to him with our thirst, our burdens, and our needs. That is exactly the point. We cannot earn the right to "eat the flesh of the Son of Man and drink his blood." We can do so only because he freely invites us.

Believe and be Saved

Prisoners, we must enter into salvation by putting our faith in Jesus Christ, by joining with him in this spiritual, personal way. If you have not put your faith in him, I plead with you to flee to Jesus, asking him for mercy. Jesus has said, "'...if you do not believe that I am the one I claim to be, you will indeed die in your sins'" (Jn. 8:24). We are lost without him. But—Praise God!— he has also said, "'...whoever comes to me I will never drive away'" (Jn. 6:37). This promise is to *whoever* comes. It is as free to you and me as it is to anyone. Our crimes and our sins do not change the promise at all. They only help us to see our need more clearly.

Saving Faith

So go to him just as you are. Go to him in all your need. Tell him that your sins have ruined you and that you are hungry and thirsty for forgiveness. Tell him that you need to escape condemnation and enter the new covenant in Jesus' blood. Eat of him and drink of him as he invites you to. Prison bars do not cage our spirits, or keep us from a personal relationship with Jesus. Go to him in faith and be saved.

Be assured, this is the will of God, and the reason that he sent his Son into this world to die. His invitation to salvation continues to the very last page of the Bible: "The Spirit and the bride say, 'Come!' And let him who hears say 'Come!' Whoever is thirsty, let him come; and whoever wishes, let him take the free gift of the water of life" (Rev. 22:17).

> "... 'I TELL YOU THE TRUTH,
> NO ONE CAN SEE THE KINGDOM OF GOD UNLESS HE IS
> BORN AGAIN.'"
> (JOHN 3:3)

CONVERSION

A Work of God

We have seen that a sinner is saved by grace through faith in Jesus Christ. This results in a personal relationship with him. It means that a person enters into the new covenant. He is forgiven of sin and becomes one with Jesus. This is a great event called *conversion*. A sinner is converted into a child of God.

Below the surface of what happens to a person in conversion is a great work of God. It was said of Lydia, "...The Lord opened her heart to respond to Paul's message" (Acts 16:14). The Lord opens the heart to make a person aware of sin, and to lead that person to seek salvation. It is this that shows him his need, and the value of Jesus Christ. It is this that leads a sinner to eat and drink of Christ so that he enters into that sinner's life.

In other words, while it is our eyes that are opened to see Jesus Christ, it is he who opens them. While we willingly join with Jesus, God is within us, making us willing. Our change in conversion is first a work of God.

Conversion is a Miracle

As sinners by nature, we are separated from God and his kingdom. We do not see him and we do not seek him. We are dead to God, spiritually, and will stay that way unless he works in us. That is what he does in conversion.

The Bible puts it dramatically. Jesus declared: "'I tell you the truth, no one shall see the kingdom of God unless he is born again'" (Jn. 3:3). "Born again" describes the work of God within a soul in conversion. As we entered into natural life through birth, we enter into spiritual life through a second birth.

Again, the Bible states: "But because of his great love for us, God, who is rich in mercy, made us alive in Christ even when we were dead in transgressions..." (Eph. 2:4, 5). "Made us alive in Christ" describes the work of God within a soul in conversion. Sin leaves us in a state of death; God gives us life.

It is written, "Therefore, if anyone is in Christ, he is a new creation; the old has gone, the new has come!" (2 Cor. 5:17). "A new creation" describes God's work within a soul in conversion. God makes us into something new, something that we were not by nature.

"Born again", "made alive in Christ", "a new creation": these terms give us the idea of a miracle within a person. The Creator freely exercises his almighty power and converts a soul.

Conversion is a Mystery

God's conversion is mysterious to men. Jesus spoke about this mystery when he said, "'You should not be surprised at my saying, "You must be born again." The wind blows wherever it pleases. You hear its sound, but you cannot tell where it comes from or where it is going. So it is with everyone born of the Spirit'" (Jn. 3:7, 8). We cannot see or explain the work of God in a soul.

Peter described conversion like this: "For you have been born again, not of perishable seed, but of imperishable, through the living and enduring word of God" (1 Pet. 1:23). The word of God works in the soul like a seed, and with the new "birth" in mind, the word of God is seen to *impregnate* the soul.

We see the Spirit and the word of God working within souls in conversion. This is much like what happened to the Virgin Mary. The angel told Mary about the miracle that God would work in her: "'The Holy Spirit will come upon you, and the power of the Most High will overshadow you. So the holy one to be born will be called the Son of God'" (Lk. 1:35). Something like that is what happens when we are converted. The Holy Spirit comes upon us, and the power of the Most High overshadows us, and impregnates our soul with the word of God. From then on the Son of God grows within us.

This is a great miracle and a great mystery. We do not understand this any more than we understand how God planted his Son in Mary. All that we see are the results. We see people that come to recognize their sin, and seek after salvation, and put their faith in Jesus Christ. We "hear its sound," but we "cannot tell where it comes from or where it is going."

Conversion is by God's Will

We may not fully understand the miracle and the mystery of conversion. But we can understand that conversion comes about by the will of God. We do not give birth or life to ourselves. We do not create ourselves. God converts us as he chooses.

The Bible explains: "In him we were also chosen, having been predestined according to the plan of him who works out everything in conformity with the purpose of his will." And, "But when the kindness and love of God our Savior appeared, he saved us, not because of righteous things we had done, but because of his mercy. He saved us through the washing of rebirth and renewal by the Holy Spirit, whom he poured out on us generously through Jesus Christ our Savior" (Eph. 1:11; Tit. 3:4-6).

He chose us. He predestined our salvation. He saved us by giving us the new birth and renewal. There is nothing of man to be found in this. It comes unconditionally, by his grace alone. God takes sinners, and by conversion, turns them into believers. It is God's gift to his chosen and predestined people. It is a miracle, a mystery of the will of God.

The Reaction to Conversion

We will not all have the same conversion experience. At times the Spirit moves like a hurricane, and at other times like a gentle breeze. We experience a miracle, yet it is a mystery.

Conversion will bring about a new life in us all. We will all see our sin and join with Jesus Christ in faith for salvation. We will set our eyes on Jesus Christ and his cross, and enter into a personal relationship with him. Our hearts will

Conversion

react to this great work of God. We will know that despite our sin God loves us. We will be humbled and amazed, but full of joy and hope. We will hate sin and have an awestruck love for God. We will praise him for his glorious grace.

Prisoners, I hope that you have known this conversion. If you have not, please think about your sin and need. You need God's great work in your life. You need Jesus Christ. You need to flee to him. Remember that he has said, "'If *anyone* is thirsty, let him come to me and drink'" (Jn. 7:37).

If you have experienced this, I urge you to think about the truth of conversion very often. There is great joy and comfort and assurance in the things we have seen. Remember that when you were dead in your sins, God came to you and miraculously gave you life by putting his word in you. He brought you to Jesus Christ and made you one with him. Remember that this means that God chose you before he made the world, and he planned your salvation in Christ. Know that he has a plan for your life now, and is working out "everything in conformity with the purpose of his will"; bars, walls, *everything!*

Think about the truth, brothers, that God Almighty loves you, and gave his Son to die for you. Love him and glorify him in return, for his amazing grace.

"'...UNLESS YOU REPENT, YOU TOO WILL ALL PERISH.'" (LUKE 13:5)

REPENTANCE

Repentance is Our Duty

We have seen that salvation from sin comes by faith in Jesus Christ. This comes freely to the needy. We do not earn salvation. However, we do have a real duty in salvation. This duty is called 'repentance', and is a part of our salvation as truly as faith is. God "commands all men everywhere to repent" (Acts 17:30). Jesus said, "'unless you repent, you too will all perish'" (Lk. 13:5). There is no salvation without repentance.

To see how repentance and faith go together, we must remember what happens in conversion. God works a miracle within us. He opens our eyes to the truth of sin and salvation, and brings us into a personal relationship with Jesus. He gives us a new life of love for God, so we begin to leave sin and to seek righteousness. He gives us both faith and repentance. "For we are God's workmanship, created in Christ Jesus to do good works, which God prepared in advance for us to do" (Eph. 2:10).

The Demands of Repentance

The best way to explain repentance may be to look at the story of the lost son. Jesus told us about a son who sinned against his father. Then he left and wasted all his money on wild living, until he was poor and hungry. "'When he came to his senses, he said, "How many of my father's hired men have food to spare, and here I am starving to death! I will set out and go back to my father and say to him: Father, I have sinned against heaven and against you. I am no longer worthy to be called your son; make me like one of your hired men." So he got up and went to his father...'" (Lk. 15:17-20).

The son came to his senses and saw the bad condition that he was in. He had sinned against his father, and he was starving. He saw that his one hope of rescue was to apologize to his father and ask for forgiveness. He had to get up and go to him.

He had to deal with two matters with his father. First, he had to deal with his sin. He had to *confess* to his father that he had sinned against him and that he was not worthy to be called his son. Second, he had to deal with his future life, if his father would take him back. He had to *commit* himself to doing his father's will.

When we come to our senses, we will see that our sin has put us in the same condition as this son. We are guilty and starving, and our only hope is to go to God. We must go to him in repentance. Like the son, we must deal with two matters. We must first deal with our sins. We must confess our sin and that we are not worthy of God. Second, we must deal with our future lives, if he will have us. We must commit ourselves to doing his will.

Confessing Sin

"Father, I have sinned against heaven and against you. I am no longer worthy to be called your son." This is what we will say if we deal honestly with our sin before God. We have no claim before God. We cannot make any excuses or deals. We go to God because we have nowhere else to go, and we hope that he will forgive us.

Jesus told another story that illustrated this. A religious man was bragging about his goodness. Next to him a well-known sinner prayed, "'"God, have mercy on me, a sinner."'" Jesus said, "'I tell you that this man, rather than the other, went home justified before God...'" (Lk. 18:13, 14). We deal rightly with our sin when we present it to God plainly, without sugarcoating, and simply beg him for mercy.

The apostle John also taught this. He said, "If we claim to be without sin, we deceive ourselves and the truth is not in us. If we confess our sins, he is faithful and just and will forgive us our sins and purify us from all unrighteousness" (1 Jn. 1:8, 9). We deal rightly with sin only when we honestly confess it before God. He knows the truth already, but if we will bring it to light, he will forgive us.

Commitment to New Life

"Make me like one of your hired men." This is what we will say if we make a commitment to live for God. We will give up our own will and ask to live by the will of God.

Jesus spoke often about this commitment. He said, "'If anyone would come after me, he must deny himself and take up his cross and follow me. For whoever wants to save his life will lose it, but whoever loses his life for me will find it'" (Mt. 16:24,25). We must no longer put ourselves first. We must put Christ first. If we do not do this, we have not repented.

Jesus also said: "'...everyone who hears these words of mine and puts them into practice is like a wise man who built his house on the rock. The rain came down, the streams rose, and the winds blew and beat against that house; yet it did not fall, because it had its foundation on the rock. But everyone who hears these words of mine and does not put them into practice is like a foolish man who built his house on sand. The rain came down, the streams rose, and the winds blew and beat against that house, and it fell with a great crash'" (Mt. 7:24-27).

The commitment that Jesus demands in repentance is to *put his teachings into practice.* We must read the Bible and learn what is right, and what is wrong, in the eyes of God. We must examine our lives in the light of these teachings, and change. We must get rid of the wrong and begin to do right. If we do not do this we have not repented. We will perish, like the house of the foolish man.

The Practice of Repentance

Prisoners, remember that the chance to repent is wonderful. We were lost in sin, but now Jesus says, "'…there is rejoicing in the presence of the angels of God over one sinner who repents'" (Lk. 15:10). There is still a chance to have everything turned around. Instead of being God's enemies we may become his friends, and heaven itself will rejoice over us!

For this to happen we must approach God and honestly confess our sins, and commit our whole lives to him. This may be costly. It may demand a public confession, or a plea of guilty and all that may result from that. We may appear weak and foolish to other prisoners, and face their insults. But if we want to be saved, we must practice repentance.

If you have been converted, you know that this is true. You have returned to your loving Father and he has joyfully received you back into his home. You know that a new life of love for God is the only right thing for you now. You cannot love him and continue to live in disobedience to him. "This is love for God: to obey His commands…" (1 Jn. 5:3).

Finally, prisoners, it might seem wrong to you to turn to God only now that you are locked up. You hear all about "Jailhouse Christians," and you can see hypocrites around you. Here is another way to look at it: If coming to prison doesn't bring you to repent, what will? Will sickness? Death? Will freedom? Do you honestly think you are more likely to commit yourself to God when you are out in the world? No, this is the time. Don't put it off because you are in prison. Your soul is at stake. Come to your senses and return to God. Confess all your sin, and commit the rest of your life to him. You will find that it is better to live in prison with God, than to live anywhere without him. Enter into the joy of the Lord.

"FIGHT THE GOOD FIGHT OF FAITH…"
(I TIMOTHY 6:12)

THE FIGHT OF FAITH

Temptation to Sin

We have seen that conversion leads to a new life of faith and repentance. Faith and repentance go together. We believe that God loves us and gave his Son to die for our sins. We believe that Jesus rose from the dead and that we will join him in eternal life. Because we believe, we follow him with our whole heart. In view of God's mercy we will offer our "bodies as living sacrifices, holy and pleasing to God…" (Rom. 12:1).

Be assured, this new life is a challenge. Our conversion does not mean that the rest of our lives will be perfect and peaceful. We are not in heaven yet. We still have sinful natures (the flesh), we live in a fallen world, and the devil leads "the spiritual forces of evil" against us. So we are tempted to doubt God; we are tempted not to live by faith. For example, God commands us to be pure, but we are tempted to think that there is a greater reward in being impure. We think about what we can have right now by serving the pleasures of sin. We think that we have more to gain by sinning than by obeying God.

Sadly, we often fall into temptation and we often sin. When we do, we feel bad. We know that we have dishonored God and that we have failed in the commitment that we have made to him. We lose the joy of salvation and the peace of fellowship with him.

Paul described this awful cycle in the seventh chapter of Romans. He said "…I find this law at work: When I want to do good, evil is right there with me. For in my inner being I delight in God's law; but I see another law at work in the members of my body, waging war against the law of my mind and making me a prisoner of the law of sin at work within my members. What a wretched man I am! Who will rescue me from this body of death?" (Rom. 7:21–25).

All believers feel this. We are tempted to sin, and like prisoners to sin, we fall and sin against the God we love. We lose our blessed fellowship with God, and we feel wretched. To believers this fellowship is more valuable than anything. We must be ready to fight to keep it. If we lose it, we must fight to regain it. We must "fight the good fight of faith" (1 Tim. 6:12).

The Battlefield of the Mind

The mind is the battlefield where we engage in this fight of faith. We have put our faith in Jesus Christ; we have "eaten" of him and entered into a personal relationship with him; we have a new standing before God. We must think about this.

This new standing before God is not based on our works, good or bad; nor is it affected even if we fall into sin. It is not based on our feelings; not even if we feel like a "wretched man." Rather, our standing is based on the work of Christ described in the gospel. God has made promises to men; he has fulfilled them by sending his Son to die on the cross for our sins and rise from the grave. In other words, our standing before God—our salvation—is based on a certain set of *facts*.

This is why the New Testament teaches so much doctrine. The facts of the gospel are doctrine. The apostles carefully recorded the facts of the life and death and resurrection of Jesus Christ, and then they carefully explained what these things mean. They wanted us to think these things through in order to live and fight in faith.

They explained that Jesus' death for our sins gives us the doctrine of justification by faith. Our sins were put on Jesus when he died, and his righteousness is now upon us. This substitution of our sins for his righteousness comes about because of God's grace. "God made him who had no sin to be sin for us, so that in him we might become the righteousness of God" (2 Cor. 5:21). We receive this righteousness by faith. "This righteousness from God comes through faith in Jesus Christ to all who believe" (Rom. 3:22).

They also explained that God's sacrifice of Christ teaches the doctrine of salvation by grace. God saves unconditionally. "For it is by grace you have been saved, through faith—and this not from yourselves, it is the gift of God—not by works, so that no one can boast" (Eph. 2:8, 9).

If we will think about these doctrines we will learn that Jesus Christ's death and resurrection makes us right with God. They teach us that God's grace towards us saves us. We will see that these things are the foundation of our faith. Even if we are tempted and fall into sin, the facts are not changed. We may fail, but God and his gospel never fail. Jesus Christ did a work and "it is finished."

The Victory

The devil is called "the accuser" (Rev. 12:10). He will tell us that we are not righteous, and that we do not deserve God's salvation. He can point out any number of sins to prove his point. He will try to rob us of our fellowship with God. But if we understand our doctrine, we can see that Jesus died for our sins, and we are righteous before God because of faith in Christ alone. We can know that although we are not worthy, God has loved us and saved us by his grace alone.

This is the victory in the fight of faith. When we are accused, we can fight past what the devil says, and even what we feel, armed with our doctrine. It is true that we fall in sin, but that is not the question. The question is: what has Christ done for us; what does God think of us? Our doctrine answers that. Christ has made us righteous. God loves us. So it is really a matter of *who* we believe. Do we believe the devil, who tells us that God does not accept us? Or do we believe God, who gave his Son for us?

This is how Paul fought in faith. He saw himself for what he was. He said, "What a wretched man I am!" But then he asked the question, "who?"—"Who will rescue me from this body of death?" And he remembered that he did not depend on himself. He depended on the grace of God and on the cross of Christ. So his next words were, "Thanks be to God—through Jesus Christ our Lord!" (Rom. 7:24, 25).

Have Faith

Fellow prisoners, I know that you have seen these things in your life. You have been tempted to doubt God, you have fallen into sin, and you have felt wretched. You have felt the

The Fight of Faith

accuser condemning you. I know that you have felt these things, because all of God's children have, just as Paul did. Take some comfort in knowing that every saint has felt this. The struggle is really a proof of your faith. After all, when you did not believe you did not care about your fellowship with God!

Don't stop with feeling wretched. Follow the example of Paul and fight in faith. Think about *who* you believe. Don't look at yourself, look at God the Father, and at Jesus Christ, his Son, and at the facts that support your faith. Get back to doctrine. God will show you that your salvation is fully in his hands. He will teach you the real glory of being justified by faith, and saved by grace. He will show you that it is not your love for him that makes you his child; it is his love for you. It is not your faithfulness to him; it is his faithfulness to you. Because of this, you will give all praise to him. You will tell yourself, the devil, and the whole world, that you trust in God and in the cross of Jesus Christ! He did not die for nothing, he died to save you from your sins!

This will restore to you your blessed fellowship with God. It will restore to you the joy of salvation. It will strengthen you in your commitment to follow Jesus no matter what. You will obey him whole-heartedly, in love and gratitude. That is the power of the cross.

> "...'All authority in heaven and earth has been given to me. Therefore go and make disciples of all nations, baptizing them in the name of the Father and of the Son and of the Holy Spirit, and teaching them to obey everything I have commanded you. And surely I am with you always, to the very end of the age.'"
> (Matthew 28:18-20)

LIVING AS DISCIPLES

Our Public Service

In the last chapter we began to look at the challenge of our new life. We face the temptation to sin. When we fall into sin we face the attack of the devil, the accuser.

That attack is private; it has to do with our own inner life with God. Our duty to God is not only private, it is also public. We have a duty to serve God among men, and the devil also attacks us in this. He is called "the prince of this world" (Jn.14:30), and to keep us from serving God he sets the "world" against us.

The term disciple explains our public duty as believers in Christ. Jesus said to the first disciples, "'Come, follow me, and I will make you fishers of men'" (Mk. 1:17), and they did. They joined him in telling the world, "'The kingdom of

God is near. Repent and believe the good news!'" (Mk. 1:15). We have the same duty.

We see this in the final command that Jesus gave to his apostles before he returned to heaven. He said, "'…Therefore go and make disciples of all nations, baptizing them in the name of the Father and of the Son and of the Holy Spirit, and teaching them to obey everything I have commanded you…'" (Mt. 28:19, 20).

The Duty of Disciples

This final command of Jesus continues today. It gives us two specific duties for disciples: be baptized, and obey Christ's commands.

When Jesus told his disciples to be baptized, he was telling them to show that they took part in his salvation. This is what our baptism is. It is a public announcement that we are "Christians." We claim conversion to Christ. "We were therefore buried with him through baptism into death in order that, just as Christ was raised from the dead through the glory of the Father, we too may live a new life" (Rom. 6:4). When we are baptized, we announce that we are joined with Jesus in death and in resurrection; we are "buried with him" (under water) and are now living "a new life" (raised up again).

When Jesus said, "teach them to obey everything I have commanded you," he was telling them that every action was important. Many of his commands are specific, with much detail. Others are general, and give broad ideas of what is expected of us. Together all of his commands make our goal to "'"Love the Lord your God with all your heart and with all your soul and with all your mind,"'" and to "'"Love your neighbor as yourself"'" (Mt. 22:37, 38). Everything that we do must show this love.

Together, baptism and obedience constitute real public service. We tell the world that we are "Christians;" that he has forgiven us of our sins and made us into new people. Then we show love to God, and to the world, as Jesus did. This will include sharing what we know of salvation with others, of course. People need to be told about sin and judgment and the gospel of Jesus Christ. They need to repent and join with Jesus by faith for salvation. As disciples we lovingly tell them about these things, and encourage them to act in faith.

The Hatred of the World

At this point the devil comes in. This can surprise us. We think that a needy, dying world will be glad to receive the good news of Jesus Christ. We think it will be glad to be loved. But the devil does not let go of his kingdom easily.

Remember, the people of the world are lost just like we once were. They do not believe in God, nor that he has a reward beyond this world. They live to serve their lusts and their pride. That is all they have. When we tell them that their sin is sin, and that they need to repent, the devil tells them that we are trying to rob them of all they have. He tells them that we are a threat; we are enemies. And they hate us.

This is to be expected. Jesus said, "'If the world hates you, keep in mind that it hated me first. If you belonged to the world, it would love you as its own. As it is, you do not belong to the world, but I have chosen you out of the world. That is why the world hates you'" (Jn. 15:18, 19). And Paul said, "…everyone who wants to live a godly life in Christ Jesus will be persecuted" (2 Tim. 3:12).

Jesus suffered. The apostles also suffered. If we are going to be disciples, we will suffer. The only way to avoid it would be to *not* announce our faith in Jesus, nor obey him. That is no option for us. We must choose to be Christ's disciples even though it means being hated by the world.

The Promises of Christ

Dare we act as disciples when it means that the world will hate us? We would not dare except for this: when Jesus gave us his commands he also gave us great promises. When he gave his final command, he also said, "'All authority in heaven and earth has been given to me.'" And, "'Surely I am with you always, to the very end of the age'"(Mt. 28:18, 20).

Do you see? Jesus Christ, who died for our sins and who rose from the grave, is the Lord of all! He has all authority in heaven and earth. He is always with us. If we will believe him, we can dare to serve him with great courage. If he says, "Be baptized," we can do it boldly. If he says, "Love your neighbor as yourself," we can obey with joy. If he says, "Make disciples of all nations," we can confidently set about changing the world, despite its hatred. The Lord Jesus Christ is with us, and he has all authority in heaven and on earth!

Overcome the World

Prisoners, if you profess to be Christians you will be insulted. If you seek to obey the commands of Jesus, you will be tested at every turn, and your love will be rejected. It may seem useless, or even dangerous, to try to make disciples of the people around you. Shame and trouble will almost surely be part of your calling. You probably know more about the world's attack than most Christians do.

Still, we must fight. We must act in faith. We must remember Jesus Christ and believe in him; trust him; hope in him. We must remember what he has done and the promises that he has made. As we act in faith, he will be with us and will act, as the Lord of all. Our profession and our love will reach some people—his people! His sheep will hear his voice and they will follow him. They will leave their sin and the world; they will repent and be baptized and learn to obey him. He will use our actions as disciples, and he will defeat the devil's efforts and the hatred of the world. As John said, "You dear children, are from God, and have overcome them, because the one who is in you is greater than the one who is in the world" and "…This is the victory that has overcome the world, even our faith" (1 Jn. 4:4; 5:4).

Finally, disciples, I would point you to Romans 8:28-38. Here Paul spoke some of the most bold and joyful words in the Bible, as he talked about overcoming the world in faith: "…we know that in all things God works for the good of those who love him, who have been called according to his purpose… If God is for us, who can be against us?… Who shall separate us from the love of Christ? Shall trouble or hardship or persecution or famine or nakedness or danger or sword? No, in all these things we are more than conquerors through him who loved us."

So Christians, forget the shame and the danger. Don't fear the devil and the attacks of the world. Believe in Jesus Christ and his promises, and have courage. He said, "'…In this world you will have trouble. But take heart! I have overcome the world'" (Jn. 16:33). One day the fight will be over, and by faith you will be a victorious disciple of Jesus Christ.

"Do you not know that your body is the temple of the Holy Spirit, who is in you, whom you have received from God?..."
(I Corinthians 6:19)

THE HOLY SPIRIT

The Spirit is a Person

In the last few chapters we have looked at the new life that we live as believers. We repent. We fight in faith against the temptation to sin and against the accusing devil. We seek to reach the world with the gospel. But we need to know that even in this new life, God is working in us, and we depend on him, not on our own strength. As Paul wrote, "...continue to work out your salvation with fear and trembling, for it is God who works in you to will and to act according to his good purpose" (Phil. 2:12, 13).

It is the Holy Spirit that is giving us the new life of faith. He is the "blessing" that God promised to all nations through Abraham (Gal. 3:14). He was promised as part of Jesus' ministry. John the Baptist said, " 'I baptize you with water, but he will baptize you with the Holy Spirit'" (Mk. 1:8). He came wonderfully on the day of Pentecost to fulfill the promise. Peter explained, "' "In the last days, God says, I will pour out my Spirit on all people..."'" (Acts 2:17).

The New Testament teaches us how to think about the Holy Spirit. He is a "he," not an "it." He is a person. He is called the "Spirit of Christ," and the "Spirit of God" (Rom.

8:9, 14). Jesus said, "I will come" and "we will come," in reference to the Spirit (Jn. 14:18, 23). So when we think about the Holy Spirit, we think of Christ and of God. The Holy Spirit is "God with us" in person, just as Jesus was when on the earth.

Christ in Us

"…From the beginning God chose you to be saved through the sanctifying work of the Spirit and through belief in the truth" (2 Th. 2:13). The Holy Spirit does the work of sanctifying us, or setting us apart for God. He sets us apart from sin, and he teaches us to "…be holy, because I am holy" (1 Pet. 1:16).

We saw the first part of his work in "Conversion." He moves in us mysteriously to give us a new birth. He comes upon us miraculously and impregnates our soul with the word of God so that the Son of God grows within us. He works in us something like the way he worked in the virgin, Mary.

This sounds amazing, yet the apostles want us to see this. More, they want us to see that Christ continues to live in us by the Holy Spirit. Paul wrote, "…God has chosen to make known among the Gentiles the glorious riches of this mystery, which is *Christ in you*, the hope of glory" (Col. 1:27 emphasis added), and, "Do you not know that your body is the temple of the Holy Spirit, who is in you, whom you have received from God?…" (1 Cor. 6:19). Christ, or the "Spirit of Christ", the Holy Spirit, lives within.

The Fruit of the Spirit

Because Christ lives in us, we "...do not live according to the sinful nature but according to the Spirit" (Rom. 8:4). Paul says, "...live by the Spirit, and you will not gratify the desires of the sinful nature" (Gal. 5: 16). Instead of living in sexual immorality, hatred, and all of the sins of our old nature, we can now live in ways that please God. We can bear the "fruit of the Spirit...love, joy, peace, patience, kindness, goodness, faithfulness, gentleness and self-control" (Gal. 5:22, 23a).

The best picture of how this occurs may be seen in John, chapter 15. Jesus calls himself the "True Vine," and us the "branches." He says, " 'Remain in me, and I will remain in you. No branch can bear fruit by itself; it must remain in the vine. Neither can you bear fruit unless you remain in me. I am the vine; you are the branches. If a man remains in me and I in him, he will bear much fruit; apart from me you can do nothing'" (v. 4,5).

Here is the work of the Holy Spirit. Like the sap in a plant that flows into the branches and gives them life, the Holy Spirit flows from Jesus Christ into believers. He is that life power that turns us from dry sticks into living branches.

How do we remain in Christ? We simply remain joined with him by faith. We remember his life, and death on the cross for our sins, and his resurrection from the grave. We believe his words and continue to trust and obey him, and love and follow him. His life pulses through us. This is the Holy Spirit. God is with us, working in us and bringing forth good fruit.

We should also hear a warning at this point. "Fruit" is the test of true faith. Jesus said, " 'By their fruit you will recognize them…'" (Mt. 7:16). If we are not bearing God's fruit in our lives, we have no reason to believe that the Spirit is in us. "…And if anyone does not have the Spirit of Christ, he does not belong to Christ" (Rom. 8:9). The Spirit within us makes all the difference.

Remain in Christ

Prisoners, test yourselves carefully and honestly to see if the Spirit of Christ is living within you. Do "love, joy, peace, patience, kindness, goodness, faithfulness, gentleness and self-control" grow in your life because of your faith?

If you can truly say that they do, consider what a wonderful blessing this is. You are a temple that God has purchased for himself at the price of Jesus' blood. He not only bought you, now he lives in you. Jesus Christ lives in you in the person of the Holy Spirit. He lives in you in order to make you holy and to bring forth fruit for God. This comes forth in our new lives, but it is not of us, it is of God. It comes forth as we remain in Jesus Christ.

What a glorious calling we have! Do you sometimes feel like your life does not have a purpose while you are locked up in prison? Please, brothers, remember that God has bought you and lives in you, and through you his holiness and fruit is reaching the world. God has put the treasures of heaven into these bodies of clay. Even from your place in prison God will give you his great blessing, will use you to share this blessing with others. So yield yourself to God; remain in Christ, and let the Holy Spirit work in you. "Do everything without complaining or arguing, so that you may become blameless and pure, children of God without fault in a crooked and depraved generation, in which you shine like stars in the universe as you hold out the word of life…" (Phil. 2:14-16).

> "'THE KINGDOM OF THE WORLD HAS BECOME THE KINGDOM OF OUR LORD AND OF HIS CHRIST, AND HE WILL REIGN FOR EVER AND EVER.'"
> (REVELATION 11:15)

THE KINGDOM OF GOD

Christ is Coming Again

Christianity is not the easy way through life. That is why only a few people choose it. As it is written, "'...wide is the gate and broad is the road that leads to destruction, and many enter through it. But small is the gate and narrow the road that leads to life, and only a few find it'" (Mt. 7:13, 14).

Why do some choose the small gate and narrow road? Christians choose to live such lives because we believe the promises of the kingdom of God. We live for the "promised land."

This kingdom is something that has been behind the scenes in all that we have seen. We lost the kingdom of God because of sin. Christ's salvation restores the kingdom to us. Now we live waiting for Jesus to come again, and to bring us completely into the kingdom of God. As He has said, "'In my Father's house are many rooms; if it were not so, I would have told you. I am going there to prepare a place for you. And if I go and prepare a place for you, I will come back and take you to be with me that you also may be with me where I am'" (Jn. 14:2, 3).

This is why we take up the new life of faith. We wait for the day when "...the Lord himself will come down from heaven, with a loud command, with the voice of the archangel and with the trumpet call of God, and the dead in Christ will rise first. After that, we who are still alive and are left will be caught up together with them in the clouds to meet the Lord in the air. And so we will be with the Lord forever" (1 Th. 4:16, 17).

Our Glorious Hope

In many ways we experience the kingdom even now. We saw this as we looked at the Holy Spirit in the last chapter. God puts Christ in us. This is "…a deposit guaranteeing our inheritance…" (Eph. 1:14). God has "…blessed us in the heavenly realms with every spiritual blessing in Christ" (Eph. 1:3). We are "…filled to the measure of all the fullness of God" (Eph. 3:19). God lives within us and lets us know his love for us. He gives us a taste of his kingdom *even* while we are here on earth. There is nothing in the world that compares to this.

But as great as our present blessing is, we have a better hope before us. We wait for the Kingdom of Glory; a place that is truly Heaven. This is beyond our minds, but the Bible gives us some sweet pictures that stir up our hearts for it.

Some of the greatest pictures of this are in the final pages of the Bible: chapters twenty-one and twenty-two of The Revelation. There we see the "new heaven and the new earth", and the "New Jerusalem, coming down out of heaven from God, prepared as a bride beautifully dressed for her husband"(Rev.22:3a). This city shines with the glory of God. It is made of pure gold. The walls are made of precious stones. Its gates are pearls. God and Jesus are its temple, and their glory gives it light. The river of the water of life flows from the throne of God. Beside the river is the tree of life. And "no longer will there be any curse."

This pictures man completely restored. The curse of death is gone. The barrier that kept us from the tree of life is gone. People are no longer separated from God. All things are restored to what they were meant to be. "'Now the dwelling of God is with men, and he will live with them. They will be his people, and God himself will be with them and be their God. He will wipe every tear from their eyes. There will be no more death or mourning or crying or pain, for the old order of things has passed away"(Rev.21:3b, 4).

Live in Hope

Fellow prisoners, what a great hope we have! Prison is not all that we will experience. This is a "present evil age"; we struggle against the "powers of this dark world"; we are "aliens and strangers in the world." But soon God will live with us. We will be his people and he will be our God. All sadness and pain will be gone forever. The old order of things will pass away. The Word will be fulfilled: "The seventh angel sounded his trumpet, and there were loud voices in heaven, which said: 'The kingdom of the world has become the kingdom of our Lord and of his Christ, and he will reign for ever and ever'" (Rev. 11:15).

Let us press on in the narrow way as disciples of Jesus Christ. When God's final trumpet sounds we will know that it was worth it. Jesus will bring us into the kingdom. Then we will truly be HOME. We will be home with God, and home with Jesus. We will be home with all of the faithful who have gone before us and with all who will come after us. We will be home forever. Alleluia and Amen!

> "'Heaven and earth will pass away,
> but my words will never pass away.'"
> (Luke 21:33)

THE WORD OF GOD

The Glory and Power of the Word of God

God reveals himself and his will to us by his word. His word tells of his glory and power. It speaks about things that no human mind could know apart from revelation. It affects us greatly: "For the word of God is living and active. Sharper than any double-edged sword, it penetrates even to dividing of soul and spirit, joint and marrow; it judges the thoughts and attitudes of the heart" (Heb. 4:12).

This word gives us new birth: "…you have been born again, not of perishable seed, but of imperishable, through the living and enduring word of God." This word gives us faith: "…faith comes from hearing the message, and the message is heard through the word of Christ." This word makes us holy: "…Christ loved the church and gave himself up for her to make her holy, cleansing her by the washing with water through the word." This word is our weapon against the evil one: It is "…the sword of the Spirit, which is the word of God" (1 Pet. 1:23; Rom. 10:17; Eph. 5:25, 26; 6:17).

Nations have risen and fallen throughout history, but the word of God has continued to spread across the earth. Ideas have come and gone, but the word of God still penetrates souls and spirits. Unlike many things that are highly thought of now, in one hundred years the Bible will still be living and active in the hearts of men. Jesus has said: "'Heaven and earth will pass away, but my words will never pass away'" (Lk. 21:33).

The Authority of the Word of God

The Holy Spirit is the one who has given us the word of God. He moved the writers of Scripture to write. "For prophecy never had its origin in the will of man, but men spoke from God as they were carried along by the Holy Spirit" (2 Pet. 1:21). God moved all of the different writers to record exactly what he wanted them to say. Over the course of fifteen hundred years, God moved forty men to write sixty-six books in different ways. Perfectly. The Holy Spirit carried the writers along so that what they wrote was "God-breathed:" "All Scripture is God-breathed and is useful for teaching, rebuking, correcting, and training in righteousness, so that the man of God may be thoroughly equipped for every good work" (2 Tim. 3:16, 17).

These writers of the word claimed to be moved by God's Spirit. They said, "…no one knows the thoughts of God except the Spirit of God," and, "…we speak, not in words taught us by human wisdom, but in words taught by the Spirit…" (1 Cor. 2:11, 13). They took this very seriously. They knew that because God was the author of the word, it had *authority* from heaven.

Because of this authority, the word is the basis for all we believe about God. We know him and his will by his word. Any question about him must be answered by it. It is our final authority. That is why Christians are always quoting the Bible. If the things that we believe about God are taught in the Bible then they are from heaven. If they are not in the Bible, then they are just from human wisdom, and there is no reason to think that they tell us about God and his will.

We must look at two questions that are often raised when we talk about the authority of our Bible in English. First, the question of translation, then, that of the "canon" of Scripture: What books should be in our Bible?

Translation

Many people dismiss the Bible by saying that whatever authority it once had has been lost in translation. After all, the earliest book of the Bible is probably over three thousand years old, and the latest is about nineteen hundred years old. It was written in other languages. None of the original writings exist. How can an English Bible in 2,001 A.D. claim to have authority from God?

First, when we talk about the "God-breathed" word of God, we are talking about the original writings: Hebrew and Greek writings that no longer exist. We don't deny that. We don't claim that every copy of those writings is perfect, or that translations into other languages are perfect. We don't say that the book in our hand is God-breathed in the same way that it was when it came from the pen of Moses or David or Paul.

However, we do say that our Bible in English has God's authority. We produce God's word in English in a way that clearly reveals God and his will. Many copies of the original writings were made which still exist. Those who honestly deal with this concern must admit that any variations between the translations are of such a nature as to have no ultimate effect on the clear teachings of Scripture.

Translation of the word of God has been studied for ages. It is not a new problem, or something that history overlooked. From the time Jesus commanded his disciples to be his witnesses "to the ends of the earth," Christians have known that the word of God must be translated. They have considered it a duty to do this carefully, trusting God to help.

Not only that, but Jesus himself used a Bible "translation." He used a Greek translation of the Hebrew Old Testament. He insisted on the authority of that translation, saying, "'...the Scripture cannot be broken'" (Jn. 10:35).

The "Canon" of Scripture

Some people question the canon of Scripture, or the *standard* of our Bible. They question what books belong in the Bible. They think that the Bible should be smaller, or larger, than it is, and that the sixty-six books of our Bible do not make up the whole word of God.

To answer this simply, our Bible is based on the standard of 'Apostolic Authority'—the authority of the apostles. Jesus Christ was "the Truth" and all that he said was the word of God. He chose the apostles, and made them his special witnesses, saying "'...when he, the Spirit of truth, comes, he will guide you into all truth...'" (Jn. 16:13). The apostles were "...those who have preached the gospel to you by the Holy Spirit sent from heaven..." (1 Pet. 1:12).

The apostles and their helpers gave us the New Testament. The New Testament confirms all of the Old Testament by its use of the Jewish Bible. The New Testament locks the Bible closed at its completion.

The Bible begins by showing us that mankind is under the curse of death and forbidden to eat the tree of life. The final chapter of The Revelation shows us that the curse of death is gone and the tree of life is given to us. Everything is made right through Jesus Christ. This is a perfect ending.

John, the last of the apostles, closes with these words: "I warn everyone who hears the words of the prophecy of this book: If anyone adds anything to them, God will add to him the plagues described in this book. And if anyone takes away from this book of prophecy, God will take away from him his share in the tree of life and in the holy city, which are described in this book" (Rev. 22:18, 19).

This standard of apostolic authority means that books that Jesus and the apostles do not support do not belong in the Bible. Other books may be good and helpful, but they must not be considered the word of God.

Further, like translation, the question of the books of the Bible is not new. From the first time God revealed his word to men, believers understood that it was their duty to share the word of God with others. This meant they had to carefully identify what was and what was not his word. The Jews and the early Christians did this. They did it openly, so that we can still see why they chose the books of our Bible, and why they rejected others.

The Conclusion

If anyone is not convinced about these things, he should study 'textual criticism' and the canon for themselves. No one should think that the Bible in English has been put together in the dark. Great care has been taken to give us the Word of God. These efforts are well documented and explained. We believe that God himself has blessed these efforts.

These questions are no excuse for denying the power and authority of our Bible. Our Bible does reveal God and his will to us. Our Bible, applied by the Holy Spirit, does give men faith and makes people holy. It is a weapon against the evil one. It does give new life. It is "…living and active. Sharper than any double-edged sword, it penetrates even to dividing of soul and spirit, joints and marrow; it judges the thoughts and attitudes of the heart." Those who deny this do so at their peril.

Stand Firm

Fellow prisoners, I urge you "…to contend for the faith that was once for all entrusted to the saints" (Jude: 3). Stand firm on the foundation of the Bible. People will try to move you off of this. They will say the Bible is an out of date book with no use for us in the twenty-first century (Democracy and modern science have all our answers). Or, it is lost to time (Maybe somewhere a secret society has the "real" word of God, but our Bible is a myth). Or, it is insufficient (We need other books to get the whole picture of God and his will). The world says only fools believe the Bible.

The people who say these things do not know the gospel of Jesus Christ. God has revealed himself to the world in his word, where he has revealed that he will save sinners through his Son. But the world does not want to know God or Jesus Christ. We should not be surprised: "'…Light has come into the world, but men loved darkness instead of light because their deeds were evil'" (Jn. 3:19), "…the message of the cross is foolishness to those who are perishing, but to us who are being saved it is the power of God" (1 Cor. 1:18).

Christians, may we love the light. May we love the message of the cross. May we love the gospel of Jesus Christ. May we always seek to know God and his will better. May we love the Bible. As David has said:

> The law of the LORD is perfect, reviving the soul.
>
> The statutes of the LORD are trustworthy, making wise the simple.
>
> The precepts of the LORD are right, giving joy to the heart.
>
> The commands of the LORD are radiant, giving light to the eyes.
>
> The fear of the LORD is pure, enduring forever.
>
> The ordinances of the LORD are sure and altogether righteous.
>
> They are more precious than gold, than much pure gold;
>
> they are sweeter than honey, than honey from the comb.
>
> By them your servant is warned; in keeping them there is great reward. (Ps. 19:7-11)

> "OH, THE DEPTH OF THE RICHES OF THE WISDOM AND KNOWLEDGE OF GOD!
> HOW UNSEARCHABLE HIS JUDGMENTS, AND HIS PATHS BEYOND TRACING OUT!
> WHO HAS KNOWN THE MIND OF THE LORD? OR WHO HAS BEEN HIS COUNSELOR?
> WHO HAS EVER GIVEN TO GOD, THAT GOD SHOULD REPAY HIM?
> FOR FROM HIM AND THROUGH HIM AND TO HIM ARE ALL THINGS.
> TO HIM BE THE GLORY FOREVER! AMEN."
> (ROMANS 11:33, 34)

GOD

God is Revealed

We saw in the last chapter that God reveals himself and his will in the "God-breathed" word. He authored the word, so it has authority from heaven. That authority is the basis for all that we believe about him.

The creation does reveal God's "eternal power and divine nature," and he has given man a conscience to reveal his law within us (Rom. 1:20; 2:15). But creation and conscience only give us a glimpse of God. Those that try to base their faith only on these things make a mistake. When they go beyond their simple beginning, they try to do the impossible. They try to figure out God on their own, but he is beyond human imagination. "'For my thoughts are not your thoughts, neither are your ways my ways, declares the Lord. As the heavens are higher than the earth, so are my ways higher than your ways and my thoughts than your thoughts'" (Is. 55:8, 9).

There is only one way to truly know God. We must leave human imagination, and trust in the word of God.

Having said that, however, we must say something more. While we know God through his word, we do *not* understand everything about him. We do not try to fit God into a box that our understanding can hold. We believe what we believe about God only because we see it in his word. We believe that his word is greater than our wisdom. Christianity honestly admits our smallness before God; he is infinitely greater than we.

Father, Son, and Holy Spirit

The best example of believing that which we do not understand may be the Christian view of God as Father, Son, and Holy Spirit. We do not understand this. We know that there can only be one God: "…God, the blessed and only Ruler, the King of kings and Lord of lords, who alone is immortal and who lives in unapproachable light, whom no one has seen or can see…" (1 Tim. 6:15, 16). We would not have imagined that this one God would be in three forms. But we see it in the Bible, so we believe it.

We see the Father. "Our Father in heaven," whose name is hallowed, whose kingdom is coming, and whose will is done.

We see the Son, Jesus, called "'…God with us'" (Mt. 1:23); called "'…my Lord and my God!'" (Jn. 20:28). We see that, "In the beginning was the Word, and the Word was with God, and the Word was God" (Jn. 1:1). In the Bible we see Jesus act in power and wisdom and judgment that can only belong to God. So we believe that he too is God, yet different than the Father.

We see the Holy Spirit who "comes down from heaven;" "goes out from the Father;" is "the Spirit of Christ" and "the Spirit of God" (Jn. 1:32; 15:26; Rom. 8:9, 14). In the Bible we see the Holy Spirit act as only God can. So we believe that he too is God, yet different than the Father and the Son.

Other passages in the Bible also show us this and sharpen the image of one God in three forms. They show us three different workers, but one will. We do not understand it, but we believe it, and we are baptized "in the name of the Father and Of the Son and of the Holy Spirit" (Mt. 28:19).

God of Our Salvation

The matter of one God in three forms is not just about theology. It is about *knowing God*; knowing him personally. It is about knowing how to look at him, come to him, and be his friend. At the beginning of this book we said that until we know the truth of sin, any religion will do. Likewise, if we just want to know *about* God, we may be able to learn something from other religions. But there is no comfort or joy in knowing *about* God if we do not *know* God.

That is why the Bible's view of God as Father, Son, and Holy Spirit is so important. As sinners we are not concerned about theology, we are concerned about salvation. In our

God we see the God of our salvation. We "…have been chosen according to the foreknowledge of God the Father, through the sanctifying work of the Spirit, for obedience to Jesus Christ and sprinkling by His blood…" (1 Pet. 1:2). We see that our God not only loved us and chose to save us, God also came to earth to redeem us by his blood. God comes into our hearts and turns us from sin to faith and holiness of life.

Our God, the God who has revealed himself in the Bible, gets to the heart of the matter. He shows us that he loves us with an amazing love and that he is the God of our salvation from first to last. So "…the grace of the Lord Jesus Christ, …the love of God, and the fellowship of the Holy Spirit…" is with us all (2 Cor.13:14).

Traits of God

When we know God as the God of our salvation, we will find great comfort and joy in everything that we learn about him. Let us begin to briefly look at what our God is like; at his traits. We will do that by reviewing this book.

Our study began by looking at "Sin." There we saw that God is *holy*. "…God is light; in him there is no darkness at all" (1 Jn. 1:5). Being holy means that he is separate from all. Everything else is created, but he alone is Creator. He is perfect, and nothing that is less than perfect can have anything to do with him.

We also saw that God is a God of *judgment* and *wrath* toward sin. "The Son of Man will send out his angels, and they will weed out of his kingdom everything that causes sin and all who do evil. They will throw them into the fiery furnace, where there will be weeping and gnashing of teeth" (Mt. 13:41,42). God will not ignore sin; his holiness demands that it be destroyed.

In looking at "Jesus Christ" and at "Salvation" we saw that God is a God of *love* and *mercy*. "For God so loved the world that he gave his one and only Son, that whoever believes in him shall not perish but have eternal life" (Jn. 3:16). He has made a way to forgive sin, while remaining holy.

In looking at "Conversion" we saw that God does his own will; he is *sovereign*. "In him we were also chosen, having been predestined according to the plan of him who works out everything in conformity with the purpose of his will" (Eph. 1:11). He acts miraculously and mysteriously to do his will.

In looking at "Repentance" and "Living by Faith" we saw that God is *righteous* and *faithful*. "If we confess our sins, he is faithful and just and will forgive us our sins and purify us from all unrighteousness" (1 Jn. 1:9). He is trustworthy.

In looking at "Living as Disciples" we saw he is *Lord of all*. "…We know that in all things God works for the good of those who love him, who have been called according to his purpose" (Rom. 8:28). He is in complete control of every event in life.

In looking at "The Kingdom of God" we saw that God is *eternal*. "… 'The kingdom of the world has become the kingdom of our Lord and of his Christ, and he will reign for ever and ever'" (Rev. 11:15). The reign of our holy God shall never end.

Think Deeply about God

Christians, this is a very brief look at our God. There is much more to learn about him. We should all be seeking to learn more every day as we read our Bibles. We should be in the habit of thinking deeply about what we read. We may read about God, and of his wrath, or his knowledge of all, or his holiness. But then we should prayerfully think about what these things mean. We should discuss what we have read with him!

Think about how these things apply to the Father, Son, and Holy Spirit. For instance, we know that God is holy; "…God is light; in him there is no darkness at all" (1 Jn. 1:5). This means that the Father is holy in heaven in creating and ruling over all things. It means that the Son is holy in offering himself for our sins, and his *blood* that redeems us is holy. It means that the Spirit is holy within us as he makes us into new creatures. Think about this.

Think about how God's holiness applies to us. A holy God has created us. Our sin has been sin against him who is holy. Our redemption is by the Son who is holy. We have been filled with the Holy Spirit. We now live in union with God who is holy, and we await the day when we shall be perfectly holy and enter into his holy kingdom.

What a blessing it is to think deeply about these things! Brothers, think about God's wrath and how this applies to you. Think about his love and how this applies to you. Think deeply about God in every way that he reveals himself to you in his word. You will soon gladly join Paul in saying:

Oh, the depth of the riches of the wisdom and knowledge of God! How unsearchable his judgments, and his paths beyond tracing out! "Who has known the mind of the Lord? Or who has been his counselor?" "Who has ever given to God, that God should repay him?" For from him and through him and to him are all things. To him be the glory forever! Amen. (Rom.11:33-36)

> "...FOR THERE IS NOTHING COVERED, THAT SHALL NOT BE REVEALED; AND HID, THAT SHALL NOT BE KNOWN"
> (MATTHEW 10:26)

NOTHING IS HIDDEN: A CONFESSION

1989

One terrible August night, in five minutes of fiery rage, I killed my wife Diane, and my mother-in-law Yolanda. After, as I returned to my senses, in an agony of sorrow and regret, I nearly killed myself as well. I wanted more than anything to undo what I had done. My dear wife and her good mother were gone and it was impossible to bring them back. Remorse, shame and fear crushed me. But I didn't have the courage to take my own life. Nor did I have the courage to turn myself in. Instead, I made the decision to cover up my crimes.

This would mean lying to everyone I knew, everyone who cared about me, all the time. It would mean living a lie. And before any of that it would mean disposing of the bodies. But this I did. I waited until the next night and I drove them out of state and hid them.

I can't begin to explain how a formerly decent and law-abiding man could come to a decision to do this. Much less can I explain how he actually carried it out! But I did. In a kind of trance, not daring to think about what I did, ignoring my conscience, I did the ugly work of disposing of bodies and beginning a life of lies. I began to carry a horrible secret that ruled my life, while my soul grew harder and harder each day.

It was after 4:00 a.m. as I returned to New Jersey after disposing of the bodies. A donut shop was the first place I found open. My nerves jangled painfully. Alcohol helped dull my mind but it didn't help my nerves. I needed to stop and rest for a minute, maybe try to eat something. I was a wreck.

The place was nearly empty; just a teenaged couple at the counter. I hid my condition as well as I could. I hoped my stagger looked like a walk. I leaned on the counter for support.

The teens giggled. I wanted to ignore them but they wouldn't give up; they wanted to be noticed. I turned and saw the boy grinning at me. Then, through his grin, he said it. It was unbelievable but true; the young man looked me in the eye and exclaimed, "Murderer!"

I nearly fainted. I was paralyzed with shock. Did I have blood on my hands? Had I left evidence on my clothes? Or did my face cry out that I had committed the most awful crime?

No; he was grinning. It was a joke. I slowly focused and saw the boy pointing. I followed his finger to the grill of my truck where a bird was hanging—dead. All the boy knew was that I'd killed a dumb bird. Unbelievable! Slowly I drew another breath. Slowly strength came back into my legs. I returned the boy's grin with something like a snarl. His grin disappeared and I took the donuts and fled.

A Confession 73

Pulling back onto the highway, the orange glow of dawn appeared before me. Another day was being born. It was beautiful; but it mocked me. That dawn sky mocked me because it explained the boy's statement—the word which had nearly floored me. And the explanation was—Almighty God! Almighty God, whose glory spread before me had sent that grinning teenager with a message as clear and as damning as any biblical prophet. Almighty God had spoken to me; he had called me a murderer. I knew that he knew and that nothing was hidden from him.

I knew it and despaired. There was only one sane course for me then. But I could not do it. The only path that made any sense at all was repentance, confessing my crimes, bringing all to light, and pleading for mercy. But I refused— God or no God, prophecy or no prophecy—my fate was sealed. I'd done the deed and nothing could undo it. So there was no point in repentance, sane or not. Sanity held no advantage that I could see. My choice had been made— much as I wished it was not—and I would take the path of insanity from that point on.

1990

I listened as the detective exposed my secret. It was unthinkable that it would be revealed; it was unbearable. I had carried my damning secret for more than a year, always afraid of, yet unprepared for, the day it should be known. And now that day appeared to be before me. Dread was being fulfilled.

The wheels in my head spun madly, seeking to analyze every word he spoke. I needed to know if he had evidence that removed all doubt. And I didn't think that I heard it. He described a weak case with little evidence—I hoped. Most importantly, he had not found the bodies. My efforts that previous August night had been successful. The heart of the case against me, the heart of my secret, was missing. Perhaps my lie might remain undiscovered. I believed that I might get up that day and walk out the door of the prosecutor's office. And if I could do that, if I could have just that much, I might stand a chance at continuing some kind of life; I might continue to breathe free.

I would have to flee of course. I would have to leave my life, my job, my friends, and my family. But I had really left my life already, hadn't I? Hadn't I left everything the day that my secret was born? I had done nothing but lie since then. I had lied to everyone about everything all the time. And that was my decision, wasn't it? I could not change it now. No. So if I got the chance I would run and I would begin telling new lies to new people in new places. That was all I had left.

However he didn't give me the chance. He finished going over my case, then he urged me to tell him what had happened. I couldn't! All I could do was squeak that I wouldn't answer questions. I said I wanted a lawyer. Then he dropped the bomb. He had already been before a Grand Jury. He had already gotten indictments against me. From somewhere he pulled a warrant ordering my arrest for two counts of murder. My last hope was crushed.

I was handcuffed and processed and taken to the county jail. Most of my memory of that day and of those that followed is hazy. Mostly I remember the worries and fears:

A Confession   75

what of my family and friends? Would I ever be with them again? Could I get out of this trouble? If not, could I survive prison?

I also remember that during that time I spent all my energy trying to look composed, to walk uprightly and without fear. I played the part (or so I thought) of a falsely accused man who was sure that the mistake would soon be cleared up. Of course it was a lie. It was the same lie, the same cover-up that I had been leading for a year. I could not give it up; it was all I had.

I continued to play-act right up until the day of my bail hearing. I went to Court hope against hope that my bail would be reduced and I would be released. But before entering the courtroom my lawyers took me aside and told me that the bodies of Diane and Yolanda had been found.

My case suddenly looked very bleak and it was obvious that I would not be released on bail. My act fell apart then and there. I was despondent. Back in my cell I began to seriously plan suicide. I hadn't had the courage to do it on the night of my crimes, but now I didn't have the courage *not* to do it. The thought of the shame of being known as a murderer along with the thought of life in prison was too much. I wanted to end it all.

On the evening that I planned to take my life there was a bang on the cell door. Surprisingly, there was a jail trustee; a large Spanish man named Angel. As he moved quickly away from the cell door, I saw that he had pushed a Gideon's New Testament under the door.

I was moved. It was the first act of kindness I had known from any inmate. I picked up the Bible and returned to my bunk. I didn't open it, however, I couldn't. I had sought God right after my crimes, filled with grief and sorrow, but he was not to be found. I knew that I was justly condemned. It was too late for me.

Later still that same night, waiting for darkness, a letter was pushed under the door. It was from my brother, and it was from his heart. The letter told of his love for me, no matter what. It also told of God's love and forgiveness. But all that I could see in my state of mind was that he did not believe my lies either. After all, why would an innocent man need unconditional love or forgiveness? If my own brother believed that I was a murderer, who would not?

I was convinced of what I must do. When the lights dimmed I knew it was time to go. I longed for the peace that would come with death. I wanted to escape the shame of what I had done and the punishment that I faced for it. I would be content to be no more—to not exist. I was ready.

I lay still for a long time to be sure the officers thought I was asleep, mentally preparing myself for the act. Then I paused to look hopefully into that black void before me.

But then ...while I did that, while I looked into that void, I became aware of something there. I became aware that it was not a void after all. I sensed something terrible there in the darkness. I suddenly experienced the greatest fear that I had ever known. The greatest fear by far. I sensed black burning coals just under my feet. I understood that the escape I planned was no escape at all. I was certain, rather, that I was on the verge of an endless torment. Also, I knew that torment was just and right because it was what I deserved for my sins. It was the perfect judgment of Almighty

God. Nothing was hidden and there was no escape from his righteous anger.

In my fear, I trembled, I wept. I absolutely changed my plans for committing suicide—suicide was not an option and must be avoided at any cost. Yet, I had nowhere else to go. I was on the edge of Hell, desperately afraid of falling in but having no way to turn back. My life had led me to that point and it still pressed me forward, threatening to push me in. It was like the whole world was rising up behind me, forcing me into the pit. It was like a mountain covered in smoke and flames, from which I heard the voice of God booming: "Thou shalt not kill." The mountain pushed me irresistibly into the fires of Hell.

Having nowhere to turn, being pressed between that terrible mountain and that place of eternal torment, I did the only thing I could. I cried out as a helpless child desperately seeking rescue; I cried from the depths of my soul, "Help, Lord!"

There in that cell, from that most low position, in answer to that desperate plea, I experienced what can only be called a miracle. It was like a ray of light coming down, burning through the black smoke of my soul. It was a glimmer of hope, a drop of love—God's love—breaking through. Even for me, even then, even there. It was like standing beside the Red Sea, watching it part before my eyes. I was shocked and amazed but I didn't hesitate. I cried again to God, begging for mercy, for forgiveness, confessing my sins, and to be made right with him. To my great joy I felt him respond in grace. The seeming smoke cleared and light increased and filled my soul. It was, I knew, the light of God coming into my life to save me.

Joy! Supreme joy! I couldn't believe it. I had thought that I would never know joy and peace again. I thought I had lost everything good and worthwhile forever. I certainly deserved to lose all! But no! As I lay there on my bunk in that jail cell I knew joy. I didn't fully understand it but I knew the love of God and the forgiveness of my sins. Peace, contentment, happiness, and hope. My troubles seemed to melt away. The punishment I still faced was nothing compared to God's love for me and eternal life with him in heaven.

My mind and heart were changed then, and I wanted to know more about God and to get closer to him. My first thought was of the Gideon's Bible, the blessed gift from Angel (how appropriate is that name?). It had been closed to me when I first received it, but that had changed. I hungered for it now.

I realized that I had not held a Bible since my parent's deaths, half of my life ago. I felt a sting of guilt, for having left God and his word back then. How foolish I had been. Still, thankfully, the past was the past and I was given a second chance at a new life. Thank God.

I opened the Bible. Not knowing where to begin I remembered my brother's letter. In it he had shared some Scripture, the parable of the lost sheep. I went to his letter and found the reference: the book of Luke, Chapter 15, and beginning with verse 4. There I turned and read these words of Jesus: "What man of you, having an hundred sheep, if he lose one of them, doth not leave the ninety and nine in the wilderness, and go after that which is lost, until he find it?

And when he hath found it, he layeth it on his shoulders, rejoicing. And when he cometh home, he calleth together his friends and neighbors, saying unto them, Rejoice with me; for I have found my sheep which was lost. I say unto you, that likewise joy shall be in heaven over one sinner that repenteth, more than over ninety and nine just persons which need no repentance."

There it was, hope for me. I believed that Jesus Christ, the Son of God, was my Shepherd. I believed that he had come into the world to save lost sinners and he had found me and I was safely in his hands. I believed he wanted me to repent and be joyfully restored to God. I most gladly repented then, promising to give my life, my all, to him forever.

I felt God smiling upon me then. Praise his name.

1991

As I began to settle in to the routine of the jail I also began facing some big questions that still nagged my soul. Of many, these three questions stood out the most:

1) How could I be forgiven of murder when God's law demanded death for a murderer?

2) How could I be changed from a terrible sinner into a man of God? And,

3) What was the end of my wife and mother-in-law? I wrestled with this terribly. I would rejoice in God, then I would think on those poor women and my joy would crash down. I needed an answer for my grief concerning them.

Slowly and gently the Lord used His Word to give me comfort and understanding in these things. I was (and I am) happy and amazed to find answers to these great questions in the old teachings of Christianity. The Bible answered my questioning soul. The God of the Bible—the Father, the Son, and the Hold Spirit—was the God of my salvation. So:

1) I could be forgiven because the Son of God died as a substitute for people who deserved death themselves, as I did. The Bible says of Jesus: "Who his own self bare our sins in his own body on the tree, that we, being dead to sins, should live unto righteousness: by whose stripes ye were healed" (1 Peter 2:24). He bore my sin, so I am dead unto sin but righteous unto God and his law.

2) I could become a changed man because the Spirit enters into the lives of believers and acts powerfully in them, working a "new birth". The Bible says: "But if the Spirit of him that raised up Jesus from the dead dwell in you, he that raised up Christ from the dead shall also quicken your mortal bodies by his Spirit that dwelleth in you" (Romans 8:11). He dwells in me and gives me a new life; he makes me able to live as dead to sin and alive to God.

3) I could trust the fate of Diane and Yolanda to God because the Father is the true and only Lord of all the earth, ruling over everything, and he was their God every bit as much as he was mine. I could bow before him and accept that in a way beyond my understanding, he always was and is and always will be on the throne. "For of him, and through him, and to him, are all things: to whom be glory forever. Amen" (Romans 11:36).

Then there was another question I faced. It was the question of what to do about my charges. I'd confessed to God, but I had not yet confessed to men. The answer was simple, of course. It was the same sane thing I'd known that awful

A Confession

August night. It was to confess my crimes, plead guilty and accept a prison sentence. But I kept hoping for God to step in and spare me. I hoped God's mercy would deliver from the consequence of my sins. So I waited and waited and time passed.

But time and waiting had their effect. The truth in my soul slowly came out. I began to see that I would have to pay the price. And at last two things brought this front and center in my life.

First there was my testimony. In the providence of God I was given opportunities to speak to other prisoners about Jesus and the forgiveness of sins and the kingdom of God. And some responded; they knew they were sinners in need of a Savior. I took this very seriously but at the same time I felt like a hypocrite for my failure to do the right thing and confess to my crimes. Where was the faith and obedience I talked about to others?

This came to a head when I was speaking to a young man crushed by guilt for what he'd done. We spoke about God and the saving work of Jesus Christ but he would not be comforted; he would not believe that forgiveness could be shown to him; he believed his sin was too great. I told him as strongly as I could that I knew God's grace was sufficient for great sinners who had committed awful crimes. I promised him I knew this from experience. He was not convinced and he put it to me directly: did I know what it was to be guilty of murder? Under the circumstances I could do nothing but tell the truth. To lie or to avoid the truth would have been a grave sin and a slap at the Lord who had shown me such mercy. So for the very first time I confessed to another person that I was indeed guilty of murder and more.

I do not know what this meant to the man to whom I spoke, but for me it opened floodgates. It became clear as day that the whole truth had to come out; I had to open the book on myself for all to read. That was the only way for me to go on, to continue with God, to know peace in my life, to serve any useful purpose. Just as I confessed to that needy man I would have to confess to all.

At about this same time another thing also moved me to make this confession. One night as I read my Bible, asking for wisdom and strength, God spoke to me. He spoke to me in his word as I read these words of Jesus: "Render to Caesar the things that are Caesar's, and to God the things that are God's" (Mark 12:17).

The words came to me with a glorious force—a gentle and beautiful and comforting power. In them I heard the still small voice of God, and I understood what the words meant for me. I knew that I owed Caesar—the state of New Jersey—for the things that I had done. The law made it clear. I knew that I had to pay that debt by accepting the sentence for my crimes. And I knew that God's love and mercy did not change that fact. I loved him and I knew he loved me, but still it was my duty to give Caesar that which I owed.

I rose from that Bible reading ready to take the steps that I had known for a long time that I must take. There was no more stalling. It was one of the most difficult things that I would ever have to do, but as enabled by the power of God and resting in his grace, I was finally prepared to go through with it.

I could barely move when the morning for my plea arrived. But while I waited to enter the courtroom, my thoughts went to the Lord Jesus Christ. I thought of his suffering; how he suffered for me, because he loved me. Yes, that was what I needed to dwell upon; that was what would help me and get me through the day.

In the courtroom at last, the judge spoke about the length of the plea agreement; of thirty years with a thirty year parole disqualifier—every single day of the thirty year sentence would have to be served. I understood it well enough.

Then came the hardest part, the point where I had to stand and tell the Court exactly what I had done. I rose and told the awful truth of those wicked, wicked murders. I acknowledged my horrible secret to the world.

The judge accepted my confession and found me guilty of two murders. But even as he did that, and as I left the courtroom and returned to my cell, I felt great relief; relief at having survived and of being alive. Even more than that, I knew then that one of the most difficult situations I would ever encounter was behind me. My nightmare, my greatest fear—the exposure of my secret—had come to pass and I had faced it and it was now over. I was amazed at the relief and peace that I felt. I realized that while many trials and dangers were still before me, I had passed through a fire which prepared me for whatever else I might have to face.

I wept with joy at this truth, and I gave thanks to the Lord with every tear. He had done it; he had brought me through in his love and power.

2008

In September of this year it has been eighteen years since I was arrested for my crimes; eighteen years spent in prison.

In writing this story now, remembering these things from my past, I have been filled again with shame for so much that I have done; for awful crimes, terrible sins. I have so many regrets. Thinking of Diane and Yolanda still brings me painful sorrow. But there are no regrets about crying out to God; repenting and seeking his forgiveness. I have no regrets about turning to Jesus Christ for salvation or calling him my Lord. I also have no regrets about publicly confessing my crimes and accepting my prison sentence. Rather, I give thanks to God for helping me to do those things. I give thanks for since that time I have been allowed to come to him freely, as his child, as his friend, accepted in the Beloved Son. And I give thanks that he has blessed and kept me, showed me grace, given me peace. The years in prison with him have been blessed beyond anything I could have imagined. I truly love the Lord.

"I love the LORD, because he hath heard my voice and my supplications. Because he hath inclined his ear unto me, therefore will I call upon him as long as I live. The sorrows of death compassed me, and the pains of hell gat hold upon me: I found trouble and sorrow. Then called I upon the name of the LORD: O LORD, I beseech thee, deliver my soul. Gracious is the LORD, and righteous; yea, our God is merciful" (Psalm 116:1-5).